SOZO – salvation, deliverance, healing, & wholeness

A Training Manual for SOZO Teams

Mike Harding

SOZO – salvation, deliverance, healing, & wholeness

Copyright © 2005 by Mike Harding (Original Edition)

Copyright © 2014 by Mike Harding

All rights reserved. No part of this book may be reproduced or transmitted in any form or by any means without written permission of the author.

ISBN 978-1500734824

Scripture taken from the New King James Version.

Copyright © 1982 by Thomas Nelson, Inc.

Used by permission. All rights reserved.

Contact information:

Pastor Mike Harding

Love Gospel Church
P.O. Box 4482
Apache Junction, AZ 85178
480.510.7089
mikecrisharding@aol.com
www.lovegospelchurch.com

For videos and audios of Pastor Mike's teachings,
go to www.xpmedia.com/channel/pmike

Table of Contents

What is sozo ministry? 1

Introducing the Rejection Tree and the Love Tree 7

The biblical basis for the five tools 11

How to use the five tools 15

Follow-up sessions 21

The Fruits of Rejection: Three Branches 23

The Fruits of the Spirit 25

Personal Spiritual Profile for Sozo 27

Breaking Agreements - Making Agreements 29

Sozo pre-appointment information 35

List and description of "root spirits" 39

Other spirits 41

What is sozo ministry?

Most people carry around a certain amount of emotional baggage from their past. Experiences of rejection, mistreatment, abuse, broken relationships and traumatic experiences all contribute to the weight of unresolved and unhealed emotional baggage. For some people, this may mean nothing more than occasional painful memories. For other people, the baggage of the past may be seriously problematic. Many people suffer with a damaged self-image, deep feelings of inferiority, insecurity, anxiety, loneliness, addictions or anger issues. These problems can affect our relationships and rob us of joy and success in every area of our lives.

If you are a Christian, the Bible says that you are a new creation. (2 Corinthians 5:17) Jesus redeemed you from your past. You are born again. But the memories and the feelings of the past may still be with you like a bad computer program, keeping you from living fully in the victory that Jesus won for you.

As Christians, we have right standing before God because of the finished work of Jesus Christ. We are saved and forgiven. We are princes or princesses of God our Father. Nevertheless, we may have emotional baggage and self-worth issues from painful childhood experiences, or from traumatic events of the past. We may look in the mirror and see an orphan rather than a prince or a princess.

When Jesus raised His friend Lazarus from the dead, *He cried with a loud voice, "Lazarus, come forth!" And he who had died came out bound hand and foot with grave clothes, and his face was wrapped with a cloth. Jesus said to them, "Loose him, and let him go."* (John 11:43-44)

This is a picture of many Christians who are raised up into eternal life through faith in Jesus Christ, but are still bound with the grave clothes of the past: old identity, old issues of rejection and emotional woundedness. What is Sozo Ministry? It is what Jesus said: "Loose him, and let him go!"

Sozo ministry was designed to help people overcome and find healing from feelings of rejection and unworthiness, fear and anxiety, anger and bitterness, and other negative emotions. Sozo is a Greek word which is usually translated in the Bible as "to save". But it means much more than simply being forgiven and someday going to Heaven. It refers to total healing, total freedom, and total wholeness in spirit, soul and body. SOZO is also translated as "to heal" or "to make whole" (Mark 5:23 and 28). SOZO ministry was designed for people who are already Christians, already born again, but who are struggling with emotional baggage from the past.

This includes our self-image and self-esteem, as well as how we relate to God and to the significant people in our lives. Sozo ministry was designed to help us in all of these areas.

(Note: There was a time when I believed that the words and concepts of self-image, self-esteem or self-worth were somehow enemies of biblical Christianity. In retrospect, I know that was because I was kind of a damaged person with deep rejection issues and low self-esteem. But God doesn't want you to hate yourself or devalue yourself. That is not humility. It is the work of the devil. Biblical Christianity means that we agree with God in everything that He thinks and says. God so loved us that He gave His only begotten Son to save us. God decided that we were worth loving and worth saving. God defined our value by the price He was willing to pay to redeem us – the life of Jesus on the cross. Biblical Christianity means that we agree with God concerning our value. When the Lord healed my self-esteem through Sozo ministry, I loved Him more, not less.)

Rejection is the number one issue for most people with emotional baggage of the past. Parental failings and experiences of abuse or neglect or mistreatment may cause deep roots of rejection and emptiness, a love deficit, a sense of worthlessness or lack of value. Once established, these roots produce bad fruit in our emotional life, our self-image, and our personality. Sozo ministry is designed to help us be healed from the roots of rejection and to replace them with roots of love and acceptance from God. This will produce good new fruit in our emotional life, our self-image and our personality.

The new birth vs. healing the soul

Some Christian leaders object to the idea of Sozo ministry. They feel that since the Bible says that we are new creations in Christ, therefore we should have no further need of anything like Sozo ministry. However, the Bible teaches that we are made up of three parts: spirit, soul and body. When you are born again, your spirit is made new now and forever. Your spirit is a new creation in Christ. However, your soul and your body are not yet made new. Your body will be renewed and resurrected at the second coming of Jesus. And before your physical body is renewed, it may need occasional healing. No Christian leader would argue that a Christian cannot get physically sick or wounded. They may go to a doctor, or they may pray for physical healing based on the finished work of the cross, but they certainly acknowledge that Christians may need physical healing. In the same way, your soul, or mind, is being renewed by the Word of God (Romans 12:2). But some Christians need healing for their wounded and damaged souls in order to really live in the victory that Jesus has won for them. James 1:21 tells us to "lay aside all filthiness and overflow of wickedness, and receive with meekness the implanted word, which is able to *save* your souls." "Save" is the Greek word "Sozo", which is also sometimes translated as "heal" or "make whole" (Mark 5:23 and 28). James is telling us that the word of God will save, or heal, our souls. He is not talking about being born again. He is addressing people who are already born again. They are already saved. He is saying that God's truth and love, imparted to us through His Word, will make our souls healed and healthy and whole. In Luke 4:18, Jesus quoted the prophecy from Isaiah 61:1 which says that He was anointed to "heal the brokenhearted." This is Sozo ministry. It is not just reeducating the mind to spiritual or religious truths. It is bringing the entire soul out of brokenness, bondage and woundedness into truth and health and wholeness. Truth will always make you free (John 8:32).

The causes and effects of rejection

Just as sin was the main element that corrupted our spirits, rejection is the main element that wounds and damages our souls.

Before accepting Jesus, our spirits were infected and corrupted by sin. It was introduced into the human race through the sin of Adam and Eve. We all inherited it. We were spiritually dead in sin. We were slaves to sin and controlled by it to some degree. But when we were born again, Jesus' death and resurrection provided us with a new spirit and the new nature. We are reborn with the good and righteous nature of God in our spirits.

But rejection is Satan's main weapon against our souls. Satan wants to convince you, as someone made in the image of God, that you are unwanted and unloved and worthless. Parents who are very damaged by sin, and who have empty and broken hearts, are usually not capable of giving their children the genuine love and affection that they need. You can't give what you don't have. Children who are raised with a lack of love, affection, safety, affirmation, motivation and forgiveness will feel rejection. They will perceive themselves as rejected. They will define themselves as rejected, unwanted and worthless. They will base their self-image and their sense of personal value and worth on these feelings of rejection. Children believe most everything they are told, good or bad. They internalize everything. If you treat a child in a way that communicates rejection to them, they will usually internalize it. They will define themselves by it. It will become part of their thought life, their emotional life, and their self-image. This is called a rejection stronghold. (2 Corinthians 10:4)

Historically, a stronghold was a castle or a fortress from which a king with his army could dominate and defend the territory around him. It was a high tower. Whoever controlled the stronghold controlled the territory around it. It works the same way in the spiritual realm. Satan wants to control and dominate every part of our lives. In order to do that, he must establish a stronghold in our minds. Through this stronghold, he can exercise a lot of control over our perceptions and our decisions. And this stronghold is its own built-in defense system. This stronghold is a lie that we believe and agree with and even defend. This stronghold is a belief that we base our lives on, even though it is against us and damaging to us. This stronghold influences or even controls much of our thoughts and our emotions and our behavior.

The very first stronghold that Satan wants to establish in a person's life is the stronghold of rejection. He wants to establish this stronghold as early in your life as possible – in childhood, in infancy, or even in the womb. If he can get you to believe that you are rejected and unwanted by the people who brought you into this world, by the people who most should love you, he can control you for life. You will internalize the rejection. You will build your self-image and your identity upon it. You will believe that you have very little worth or value. Your will is weakened. With this stronghold in place, it is an easy matter to bring in other strongholds such as fear, anger, pride, jealousy or suicide. The list is endless. With the rejection stronghold firmly controlling your soul, you become almost a puppet for Satan. Even as a born-again Christian, Satan can manipulate you with thoughts and feelings of rejection. As soon as you decide to rise up and move forward in God, Satan hits the "replay" button in the rejection stronghold in your mind, and most of the time he can knock you back down again.

What sozo ministry is…

Sozo ministry recognizes the rejection stronghold as one of the most dangerous enemies of your soul. Sozo ministry uses biblical tools and truths to pull up the root of rejection, and helps you replace it with the truth and the genuine experience of God's love for you. Using the five tools of forgiveness, inner healing, repentance, deliverance and truth therapy, Sozo ministry helps you to proactively uproot and overcome the old, damaged identity and build a new identity as a beloved son or daughter of God. It helps you to transform your thought life, your emotional life and your personality by receiving and experiencing God's personal love for you.

And what it is not

Sozo ministry is not a magic wand. It is a process. It is a process that you must cooperate with and participate in. Old strongholds do not go away easily. There is an element of spiritual warfare to this process. You must want to be whole and healthy, and you must be willing to pursue it and fight for it. You cannot hold onto victim status and gain your freedom. Sozo ministry identifies where the wounds of rejection came from, but responds with forgiveness and healing rather than blame or victim status. We are overcomers and conquerors in Christ. Someone wisely once said, "I am not going to work harder for your freedom than you are." Sozo ministers are experienced guides. They can lead people into the process of healing and wholeness, but they cannot wave a magic wand over them. Jesus said, "You shall know the truth, and the truth shall make you free." He also said, "If you abide in My word, you are My disciples indeed."

Introducing the Rejection Tree and the Love Tree

In this booklet there are two tools, or diagrams. The first diagram is called the Rejection Tree, and the second diagram is called the Love Tree. These diagrams are symbols of our souls. The Rejection Tree represents a soul under the influence of a rejection stronghold. The Love Tree represents a soul that is rooted and grounded in the love of God. (Please contact me through LoveGospelChurch.com for larger master copies of these tools.)

Every tree has an underground, invisible root system and an aboveground, visible system of branches and fruits. The roots of the Rejection Tree represent our past experiences of rejection or hurt or abuse. The three branches represent the resulting emotions and behaviors that people around us experience and see. What the people around us usually cannot see is our root system - our past experiences that caused our negativity. They only see how we talk and act now. These three branches of the Rejection Tree are Internalized Rejection, Externalized Rejection, and Attempts to Compensate. Internalized rejection basically means self-rejection. We learn to agree with the idea that we are rejected and worthless. This can manifest in low self-esteem and insecurities and social withdrawal, and can eventually even lead to suicide, the ultimate form of self-rejection. Externalized Rejection basically means that we are responding to the hurt with anger and hardness of heart. This also may take other forms such as pride and rebellion and an out-of-control temper, and may even lead to murder as the ultimate form of externalized rejection. Attempts to compensate basically means that we try to "super-perform" in order to prove our worth to ourselves and to others, or we may use artificial substitutes for love because we don't have enough of the real thing. Attempts to compensate often produce religious performance also.

In the Sozo ministry session, we will use the Rejection Tree as a tool for diagnosis and for healing. We will also use the Love Tree as a vision-caster for what our souls can become when they are rooted in God's love.

Personal Spiritual Profile

Also included in this book is a sheet called the Personal Spiritual Profile, which has four questions. The first two questions are designed to help the Sozo team determine if a person they are ministering to – let's call him or her the client - has participated in cults, false religions or occult activities. This is extremely important to know, as these things are usually an "open door" to demonic spirits and must be dealt with during the Sozo session. The third question on the profile asks about experiences of emotional trauma. This will be necessary information when you pray for inner healing and deliverance, because trauma is often an open door to spiritual oppression, especially the spirit of fear. The fourth question explores if there is anyone or anything more important than God in the client's life. Jesus said to seek first the kingdom of God, and everything else will be added. This question helps the client to examine and rearrange his/her priorities, if necessary.

Sozo teams

Sozo teams help people find personal wholeness and overcome hindrances or obstacles to their spiritual growth and progress, primarily through inner healing and deliverance. A Sozo team will usually consist of two people who are trained in Sozo ministry. Jesus sent out ministry teams in twos. This is a built-in safeguard against people misquoting or misrepresenting anything that was said or done during the ministry session. As much as possible, Sozo team members should be spiritually mature and should have a balance of compassion and strength. A mercy gift is valuable in Sozo ministry because we don't want a person to leave feeling more rejected than when they came in! However, strength and directness is needed to lead the client out of a victim mentality and to help them proactively deal with their issues. One of the team members should be the agreed-upon leader of the session. To avoid any kind of disorder, he or she should lead the majority of the session. Usually, this person will be the one with the most experience in Sozo ministry, unless the secondary team member is being trained to lead. The second team member may complement the ministry session, but should not dominate it. The second team member should also offer silent prayer backup. Sozo teams will use 5 basic spiritual tools: **forgiveness, repentance, deliverance, inner healing and truth therapy**. The purpose of this manual is to guide Sozo team members in how to understand and use these basic tools.

Sozo session guidelines

A Sozo team should plan to spend from one to three hours with a client to help him/her identify obstacles to their spiritual growth, to remove the roots of those obstacles, and to begin the healing process. The ministry location should be comfortable and have a sense of privacy and safety. Childcare, if necessary, should be provided outside of the Sozo session. It is very difficult for a client to fully participate in a Sozo session with a child present, with the possible exception of a small infant. It is important that clients seeking sozo healing be as open and honest with the Sozo team members as possible. Realistically however, clients will become more open and honest as they move forward in healing and as they gain trust for the Sozo team members. Several meetings with the Sozo team may be needed for a person to make really good progress. Team members should gently challenge a client to be open and honest, but should never push them or pressure them beyond where they are emotionally prepared to go. Sometimes people are not initially ready to face the fear of deep traumas or to deal with issues that cause tremendous shame. Pressuring them would break trust, and it would be counterproductive. Obviously, it is also vital that Sozo team members treat all information shared by the client as private and confidential.

The biblical basis for the five tools

FORGIVENESS

Bible verses: Matthew 6:12-15, Matthew 18:15-35, Mark 11:25-26, Luke 23:34, John 20:21-23, Ephesians 4:32

Applicable Principles: The principle in these passages is that if we refuse to forgive others their sins against us, we are refusing to do for others what God has already done for us through Christ. God forgives and forgets; Satan remembers and accuses. Who should we agree with? If we refuse to forgive others, we are maintaining an agreement with Satan and thus giving him a form of legal authority over us to hold us in bondage and torment. (See Matthew 18:21-35.) If we freely forgive others as God freely forgave us in Christ, we take away Satan's legal ground to control us, we are in agreement with God, and we open the channel for God's healing power to flow into our hearts and souls.

Note #1: It is usually not effective to issue a blanket statement like, "Well, I just forgive everyone." It is usually necessary to examine our hearts for specific resentments and specific hurts involving specific people and events, and then to forgive those specific people for the specific offenses. It is also very effective to forgive people for "the way you made me feel". Offenses are often very subjective. We receive personal healing and freedom through proactively forgiving, regardless of the other person's actual motive or intent.

Note #2: For years I taught, based on Matthew 6:15, that if we would not forgive others, God would not forgive us either. I continued to teach that until the Holy Spirit told me that I didn't know what I was talking about. He led me to Ephesians 4:32, which says that we should forgive because we have already been forgiven in Christ. What Jesus said was true when He said it. What Paul wrote was true when he wrote it. *The cross changed everything!* We forgive (1) because we have been forgiven and, (2) so that we can eliminate any point of agreement with Satan and (3) so that we may freely receive the flow of God's healing for ourselves and others.

INNER HEALING

Bible verses: Isaiah 61:1-3, Luke 4:17-19, James 1:21

Applicable Principles: The greatest cause of a "wounded soul" is rejection. People suffer rejection when they are unloved, unwanted, unprotected, unappreciated, abused, or mistreated by people who should have loved, protected and valued them. Many of these wounds happen in childhood when people are most vulnerable. Often, parents who have been emotionally wounded will themselves cause wounds of rejection in their own children. People who never find inner healing may spend their entire lives looking for wholeness, while always feeling somehow inferior and incomplete. Jesus came to "heal the brokenhearted", to heal the inner man, so that people can be whole and fulfill their God-given destinies. James speaks of "saving the soul". The word "save" is the Greek word "sozo", which means the full healing and wholeness of the entire person, spirit, soul and body. Sozo team members will pray for inner healing because Jesus is the Healer. Prayer for inner healing is most effective after forgiveness has been extended to those who caused the wounds of rejection.

REPENTANCE

Bible verses: Matthew 4:17, Romans 6:16, Colossians 2:13, James 5:16, 1 John 1:9, Psalm 32, 2 Chronicles 7:14

Applicable Principles: Sin is what caused mankind to fall from right relationship with God, to fall from their God-given dominion, and to become spiritual slaves of Satan. Jesus took the power and the consequences of our sin on the cross, but that still leaves the ball in our court, so to speak. We must honestly face our sins, confess our sins to God, and repent, seeking to do what is right in God's eyes and stop hurting or damaging others. When we maintain an agreement with sin, we give Satan an open door, a "legal" entry point. When we confess and repent, when we put sin under the blood of Jesus, Satan loses his legal ground and we walk fully in our God-given dominion. This tool is very important because people who have been victimized or abused by the sin of others often become victimizers themselves, even though they may continue to see themselves primarily as victims. Rejected people often reject others. Abused people often abuse others. To find wholeness, we must honestly face reality if we have allowed our pain to justify causing pain to other people.

DELIVERANCE

Bible verses: Luke 6:17-19, Luke 8:1-3, Luke 13:10-13, Matthew 10:1, Mark 16:17, Acts 16:16-18, Acts 19:11-20, Genesis 4:7

Applicable Principles: Evil spirits (fallen, rebel angels) seek to oppress and torment people and even gain access into their souls and/or bodies. They gain entrance through "open doors": our agreements with sin, our agreements with unforgiveness, our participation in any occult activity, our experiences of sexual victimization, abuse or other traumatic events, and sometimes even through generational curses (the sin of our ancestors). They cause fear and torment, they hinder spiritual growth, and they drive people towards further sin and bondage. They perpetuate mental deceptions and even affect people's personalities. Jesus set people free from evil spirits by commanding them to leave. He gave us the same commission and the same authority. Usually, to permanently set people free, we must help them identify and reverse the "open doors" of sin, unforgiveness, trauma, generational curses, etc.

Note #1: Can a Christian have a demon? Can a demon live in the same place as God? My understanding is that if we are born again, the Holy Spirit primarily resides in our spirit. I'm certain that no demon can gain entrance to our spirit. However, our soul and body seem to be accessible to demons, especially as we maintain points of agreement with them. Whether you want to see it as "casting out demons" or simply breaking agreement with them and making them leave, the result is the same: freedom.

TRUTH THERAPY

Bible verses: James 1:21, Romans 12:2, John 8:31-32, 2 Corinthians 10:3-5, Ephesians 4:20-24

Experiences of rejection and trauma, critical words, and the whisperings of evil spirits cause people to believe lies. Once we embrace the lies, they become enemy strongholds. Many people's self-image, as well as their entire belief system, is based on lies that the devil planted in their minds to cripple and defeat them. People must "renew their minds" with the truth that is found in God's word. Their entire identity and self-image must be reconstructed with the truth of how much God loves and values them. General Bible knowledge is usually not enough. Specific lies and mental "strongholds" of the enemy must be torn down and replaced with specific truths from God's word. This will be a process and requires perseverance.

How to use the five tools

Begin to apply the five tools in this order: forgiveness, inner healing, repentance, deliverance, and truth therapy. However, I have found that you will have to use these tools like the five strings on a guitar: you will use them over and over, in different combinations, as needed. There will be lots of overlap and interconnection.

BEGINNING THE SESSION

Begin with prayer. Ask the Holy Spirit to come in His manifested Presence, to bring healing and freedom, to guide everyone present, and to reveal buried issues that need to be addressed in this session.

At this time, introduce the Rejection Tree and the Love Tree. Explain that the trees are symbols of our souls when rooted in rejection or in the love of God. Explain the symbolism of the root systems and the branches.

Also introduce the Personal Spiritual Profile now. Explain its purpose, and ask them to fill it out. (Or, an alternative is to send your client a package before their appointment which contains a Pre-appointment Information Sheet, copies of the Rejection Tree and the Love Tree, and a Personal Spiritual Profile. All of these are included in the Appendix section of this book. You might ask your client to fill out the Profile in advance.)

APPLYING FORGIVENESS

Interview your client, asking them to identify all their significant resentments, emotional wounds, hurts, disappointments, bitterness, etc. They must identify the people who caused these hurts and resentments, as well as describing the cause. Were they abused? Betrayed? Abandoned? Did someone fail to love them, protect them, or value them? Were they bullied or criticized? Who do they blame for their problems? Whose name or face still causes them pain, fear, or anger? Write down each name and the associated cause at the roots of the "Rejection Tree" diagram. Also, refer to the Personal Spiritual Profile and identify any traumatic experiences listed there. It will be necessary to forgive any person responsible for causing rejection or trauma. After identifying the people and the causes of their pain or anger, share the Bible verses and the principles of forgiveness. Short personal testimonies are also very helpful. Now lead them in prayers to forgive each person who has caused them pain or resentment. The prayers should be specific, naming the people and the events that need forgiveness. Note: sometimes people try to forgive "on the surface", because the memory is very painful or frightening. Encourage the person to "go deep" and forgive from the place of pain, not just on the surface. They should say something like, "I forgive you, _____(name)_____, for _____(the specific offense)_____, in Jesus' name." Sometimes, instead of a specific event, the person will need to forgive the offender for a pattern of behavior, for the way they made them feel, or for the effect they had on them. They may want to pray something like this: "I forgive you, _____(name)_____, for making me feel _____." You may need to help them understand that forgiving is an act of the will, and not necessarily a feeling or an emotion. The feeling of having forgiven may come later; the act of the will must be done now as an act of obedience to God. This portion of the Sozo session is often the longest. No shortcuts should be taken here.

APPLYING INNER HEALING

Now it's time to pray for inner healing. This process should not be rushed in any way. Team members should refer to the roots on the Rejection Tree diagram, and to anyone who was a cause of trauma from the Personal Spiritual Profile. Systematically pray through each painful or traumatic event, each painful relationship, and each rejection experience, asking Jesus to heal that place in the person's heart and soul. Ask Jesus to visit that memory and transform it with His Presence. Ask the Holy Spirit to pour in God's love and healing power. Ask the Lord specifically to fill any place in the person's heart and soul that was previously occupied or controlled by rejection. During this process, there are a couple of tools or principles that are particularly powerful and effective. First of all, take time to pray over *each* painful memory, and then just *wait* for a while, praying softly in the Spirit. Allow God time to begin a healing in that area. Don't rush it! Secondly, *ask God to speak to the person*. Ask Him to speak whatever He wants to say to them regarding that event or memory... and then *wait quietly*! Frequently, the Lord will speak something to the person, or show them a vision, that will bring healing or a new perspective in a moment's time. Jesus really is the Healer of the brokenhearted!

It is also very helpful to pray specifically in response to the kind of woundedness that you are seeing in the client. For example, many people have father wounds; it is very common. If your client has rejection issues from his/her father, pray that God would minister His Fatherly love toward them. Pray that God would reveal Himself as their loving Father and that He would give them a new identity as a beloved son/daughter. *Then wait on Him and let Him do it.* Or, if your client suffered a sexual violation, pray that Jesus would wash away any sense of shame or defilement and restore them to a sense of purity. The Holy Spirit will guide you in how to pray.

APPLYING REPENTANCE

Now have the client look at the branches on the "Rejection Tree" diagram and identify any attitudes or behaviors that he/she has developed in response to the roots of rejection. Discuss and identify how these attitudes and behaviors are either the product of rejection (fear, insecurity, inferiority, escapism) or attempts to overcome or compensate for the feelings of rejection (anger, pride, rebellion, control, perfectionism, competition, etc.). Have them circle their attitudes or behaviors on the branches of the tree. Also, ask them to describe to you any of their behavior that is hurtful or damaging to other people, especially their family members and loved ones. (The victimized often become victimizers without realizing it.) Also at this time, refer again to the Personal Spiritual Profile. The profile identifies dangerous "open doors" that must be closed: cults, false religions and occult activities. The profile also identifies any need for rearranging spiritual priorities, i.e. putting God first. Finally, ask them to identify and describe any other sin issues that they have struggled with, that they need to confess and bring to the cross.

Now lead the client in specific prayers to confess everything that they have identified as sin. These prayers should be as specific as possible. They should take personal responsibility for the wrong behaviors and attitudes, asking God for forgiveness and for the grace to overcome them.

Note #1: Your client may not be sure which items from the branches of the tree should be included in repentance. Some things are clearly matters of repentance, like pride or rebellion, for instance. Other items are less clear. Should you repent for being fearful? A guiding principle is: the more you can take responsibility for something, the more victory you will have. However, the more you claim victim status and helplessness, the less victory you will have. Jesus said many times in the scriptures, "Do not fear." So, if you take that as a command, and if you choose to take responsibility and repent of fear, you will have more victory. Your choice.

Note #2: When confessing any kind of occult activity or false religion, have the person verbally renounce and reject each and every occult connection or practice in the name of Jesus. Have them ask forgiveness for themselves and for any family members who were involved. These "open doors" must be solidly closed, and any associated spirits cast out during the deliverance session. Finally, ask them to pray a prayer of commitment, putting God first in their lives.

APPLYING DELIVERANCE

Deliverance is the next step. We have already seen from the above scripture references that Jesus cast out a "spirit of infirmity", and Paul cast out a "spirit of divination". There are also Bible references to a "deaf and dumb spirit", an "unclean spirit", a "spirit of fear", a "jealous spirit", a "perverse spirit", an "antichrist spirit", and many, many others. So we can conclude that evil spirits (rebel angels) can be identified by the work they do, the sins they promote, or the specific kinds of torment they cause. We also read that Jesus cast seven evil spirits out of Mary Magdalene, presumably while Jesus was taking her through some kind of inner healing and deliverance process. So now we will minister deliverance. We will use the list of sins and the fruits on the rejection tree to identify what spirits we are likely dealing with. Some of the attitudes and behaviors on the list will be spirits. Others will simply be mental "strongholds" that need to be overcome with repentance and truth therapy. Nevertheless, we will address everything on the list as if it were a spirit. (Better safe than sorry.) In addition, you can refer to the list of root spirits and their descriptions at the end of this manual. Review the list, asking the person to identify any spirits that are possible targets for this deliverance session. Finally, ask the Holy Spirit to give the Sozo Team members words of knowledge and the gift of discerning of spirits to identify anything that might have been overlooked. Then, begin the deliverance time. Ask the person to repeat the commands after you. (You want them to exercise their will against the enemy spirits.) Have them say: "Spirit of _____, I command you in Jesus' name to leave me!" Do that for each spirit on the list. (Again, better safe than sorry!)

Note #1: Always cast out the spirit of rejection. It is the major stronghold we are dealing with. Also cast out its cousins "fear of rejection" and "perceived rejection".

Note #2: If your client has been involved in the occult in any way, have him or her cast out the spirits of divination and witchcraft. Divination means getting supernatural guidance or communication from any source other than God. Witchcraft means exercising supernatural power or control by any source other than God.

Note #3: If your client was involved in any cult or false religion, have him or her cast out the spirit of antichrist and any religious spirits that counterfeit the work of the Holy Spirit.

Note #4: Often times, you will have virtually no manifestations during deliverance. However, sometimes there may be manifestations as evil spirits leave, or as they fight to hang on. These manifestations can range from very mild to quite strong, depending on their strength and the degree of control they have had in the person's life. Sometimes there is simply the "sense" of something leaving, with a feeling of lightness, joy or release afterwards. Sometimes there are manifestations such as yawning, coughing, or muscle tightness while spirits are leaving. Sometimes, the person will become incapable of repeating the command because the spirit begins to manifest and take control of them. Occasionally, the spirits will speak through the person and try to defy you. In this case, the Sozo team members should simply take greater control and directly command the spirit to come out. In very extreme cases, the person being delivered may scream, shake, fall down, or even vomit while being delivered. If the spirits want to argue or manifest a lot, the team members should use appropriate authority and command them to be bound, quiet, and come out immediately. *In all cases and at all times, treat the client with great honor and respect, and encourage them to participate with their own will and authority as much as they can.* End the deliverance time with a prayer that the Holy Spirit would heal and fill any places that were previously occupied by enemy spirits. Administer the baptism in the Holy Spirit if needed. Close with thanksgiving and worship.

APPLYING TRUTH THERAPY

The final step in the process is truth therapy, also called renewing your mind. Included at the end of this book is a set of pages called "Breaking Agreements and Making Agreements". With your client, read through the Scripture verses and promises that apply to healing the soul. Then lead your client through the prayers to break agreement with the lies of rejection and come into new agreement with the truth of God's love. You will want to do this together in the Sozo session, but you will also send the "Breaking Agreements and Making Agreements" pages home with your client for follow-up "homework". Encourage them to use these prayers daily for weeks or months, until they feel that they are walking in truth and victory. This is a process that requires perseverance because Satan hates to lose control over anyone, and he will fight to regain that control. In addition, our minds are creatures of habit. Old programming takes time to change. We must fight through to victory, transforming our minds with God's truth.

Follow-up sessions

It may be necessary to have follow-up sessions with people. Many times they are not spiritually or emotionally strong enough to deal with all their issues at once. Sometimes people find deliverance and healing in one area at a time. As they take control of this new territory, they become ready to advance some more.

Q and A

Q – Can we minister physical healing during these sessions?

A – YES! Physical healing is sometimes connected to repentance, deliverance, and the resolution of emotional issues (inner healing).

Q – Can we give people advice on personal issues and decisions during these sessions?

A – Avoid it. Stick with scriptural principles that apply to everyone. Encourage them to seek God for their own decisions. If you help them make a personal decision, you somehow become responsible for the outcome…and you don't want that!

Q – Can we share other people's stories and testimonies during these sessions to help build faith and understanding of the healing process?

A – Yes, if you don't reveal people's identities or other compromising details without their permission.

Q – What can we do for people who have nightmares?

A – Nightmares are almost always an indication of a spirit of fear at work. Ask questions - look for the "open door". Did they suffer some traumatic event? Did someone or something cause them to feel deep fear as a child? Command the spirit of fear to get out, and pray for inner healing from any traumatic or fearful memories.

Q – Should we give people our home phone numbers and allow more personal support outside of these sessions?

A – You may if you choose. Use your best judgment.

Q – What if we run into something bigger than we can handle?

A – Refer the situation to a pastor or other leader.

Q – What if someone seems to not be making good progress?

A – Pray for them and encourage them. You may even feel led to fast for their breakthrough, but don't carry the whole load for them. Each person is responsible for their own level of motivation, honesty, and perseverance.

The Fruits of Rejection: Three Branches

The Fruits of Rejection: Three Branches

Internalized rejection strongholds
perceived rejection, fear of rejection, low self-esteem, poor self-image, **inferiority,** insecurity, inadequacy, sadness, grief, sorrow, self-accusation, self-doubts, condemnation, fear of failure, fear of others' opinions (fear of man), depression, **fear,** anxiety, worry, negativity, pessimism, hopelessness, despair, withdrawal, guilt, eating disorders, sleep disorders, self-cutting, **suicide**

Externalized rejection strongholds
refusing comfort, rejection of others, harshness, hardness of heart, skepticism, sarcasm, defiance, inability to trust unbelief, aggression, suspicion, envy, jealousy argumentativeness, stubbornness, **pride,** foul language, **rebellion,** contention, controlling spirit, manipulation, bursts of temper, sexual aggression, verbal, emotional, physical or sexual abuse towards others, fighting, violence, rape, anger, hatred, accusations, revenge, **murder**

Attempts to compensate
striving, overachievement, **selfish ambition,** delusions of grandeur, lustful fantasies, sex as a substitute for love, food as a substitute for love, competitiveness, envy, jealousy, independence, possessiveness, perfectionism, OCD (obsessive-compulsive disorder), hoarding, critical, judgemental, comparing, religious spirit, Pharisee spirit, pride, egotism, manipulation, control, self-protectiveness, self-justification, self-idolatry, willfulness, self-centeredness, power trips, haughtiness, **performance orientation,** approval-seeking, religious legalism

The main stronghold - spirit of rejection
+ perceived rejection
+ fear of rejection

The Rejection Tree
rejection affecting the whole personality

The Roots of Rejection

Possible roots (causes) of rejection
All children need: 1. unconditional love 2. Security and protection 3. Acceptance 4. Value as a person 5. Forgiveness of mistakes 6. Motivation to reach potential 7. Affirmation and praise for accomplishments. If a child's father or mother or other parental figure fails to meet any or all of these needs, there may be some root of rejection. Other possible causes: being given up for adoption, mistreatment, abuse, neglect, sexual violation, betrayal, adultery, divorce, suicide of a loved one, alcoholism or drug addiction in the home, severe financial instability, being an unwanted child, being the "wrong" sex, not bonding with a parent, violence or tension in the home, family history or heredity of rejection, mistreatment by teachers or schoolmates, excessive criticism, inability to gain approval of father or mother, bullying, abuse by a spouse, betrayal by a minister or other authority figure, birth defect, being born "different" in some way, etc.

List here your roots of rejection
(the person and the cause)

The Fruits of the Spirit

The Fruits of the Spirit

Internalized love

"Yes, I have loved you with an everlasting love..." Jeremiah 31:3

...the love of God has been poured out in our hearts... Romans 5:5

Externalized love

We love Him because He first loved us.
1 John 4:19

Freely you have received, freely give.
Matthew 10:8

This is My commandment, that you love one another as I have loved you.
John 15:12

But the fruit of the Spirit is love, joy, peace, longsuffering, kindness, goodness, faithfulness, gentleness, self-control.
Galatians 5:22-23

Resting by faith in the finished work of Christ

...to the praise of the glory of His grace, by which he made us accepted in the Beloved.
Ephesians 1:6

Sabbath rest, entered by grace
Hebrews 4:1-10

The Love Tree
God's love affecting the whole personality

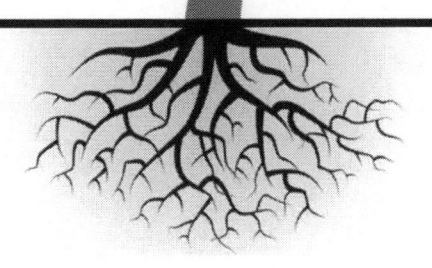

...that you, being rooted and grounded in love... may be filled with all the fullness of God.

Ephesians 3:17-19

...having predestined us to adoption as sons by Jesus Christ to Himself...

Ephesians 1:5

The Roots of God's Love

Personal Spiritual Profile for Sozo

This profile is an additional tool – a supplement to the Rejection Tree. It will help you identify ways that you or your family may have opened the door to spiritual oppression. It will also help you identify areas of emotional trauma or spiritual priorities that may need attention.

1. Have <u>you</u> or has any person in your family been involved in any cults or false religions?

    ___ Hinduism   ___ Islam

    ___ Baha'i faith   ___ Jehovah's Witnesses

    ___ Buddhism   ___ Unity

    ___ Mormonism   ___ Christian Science

    ___ devotion to Mary, saints, or religious images   ___ Masons and Masonry

    ___ any religion or teaching that denies the deity of Christ and salvation through faith in His death and resurrection (Please describe) _____

    ___ any church that is excessively authoritarian or controlling of your personal life

2. Have <u>you</u> or has any person in your family been involved in any occult practices?

    ___ calling the dead or other spirits   ___ ESP, mind reading

    ___ horoscopes and astrology   ___ New Age, crystals

    ___ psychics/palm reading/fortune telling/tarot cards   ___ satanism

    ___ magic or good luck charms   ___ Ouija board

    ___ Dungeons and Dragons   ___ superstitions

    ___ witchcraft or sorcery (including white magic)   ___ hypnotism

    ___ astral projection/out-of-body experiences   ___ spirit guides

    ___ Transcendental Meditation/Eastern meditation   ___ secret ceremonies

    ___ other (Please describe)_____

3. Have you personally experienced emotional trauma in any or the following ways?

___ verbal, emotional, physical, or sexual abuse   ___ abandonment

___ rape or sexual aggression   ___ death of a loved one

___ violence   ___ abortion or miscarriage

___ breakup of marriage or family   ___ near-death experience

___ severe injury   ___ car accident

___ victim of a crime (please describe) _____

___ any fear or phobia inducing experience (please describe) _____

_____

___ other (please describe) _____

_____

4. Is there anything or anyone in your life that is more important to you than God? Is there anything or anyone in your life that would cause you to not walk in victory with God? What or who is it? Are you willing to change your priorities and put God first in your life?

Breaking Agreements - Making Agreements

These pages contain Bible verses and promises that will help you to break agreements with unhealthy lies and come into agreement with God's truth. These verses address the root system of rejection as well as the three branches on the Rejection Tree. Please read and re-read these words and promises from God. And please use the prayers for breaking and making agreements. Use them often - even daily - until you know that you are walking in victory and love!

Root System - <u>The Seven Needs</u>

1. Unconditional love - Ephesians 2:4 - But God, who is rich in mercy, because of His great love with which He loved us...

Jeremiah 31:3 - The LORD has appeared of old to me, saying: " Yes, I have loved you with an everlasting love; Therefore with lovingkindness I have drawn you.

Mark 1:11 - Then a voice came from heaven, "You are My beloved Son, in whom I am well pleased."

John 17:23 - I in them, and You in Me; that they may be made perfect in one, and that the world may know that You have sent Me, and have loved them as You have loved Me.

2. Security and protection - Psalm 4:8 - I will both lie down in peace, and sleep; For You alone, O LORD, make me dwell in safety.

3. Acceptance - Ephesians 1:6 - to the praise of the glory of His grace, by which He made us accepted in the Beloved.

4. Value as a person - Matthew 6:26 - Look at the birds of the air, for they neither sow nor reap nor gather into barns; yet your heavenly Father feeds them. Are you not of more value than they?

Ephesians 1:18 - that you may know what is the hope of His calling, what are the riches of the glory of His inheritance in the saints

Deuteronomy 7:6 - For you are a holy people to the LORD your God; the LORD your God has chosen you to be a people for Himself, a special treasure above all the peoples on the face of the earth.

5. Forgiveness of mistakes - Ephesians 4:32 - And be kind to one another, tenderhearted, forgiving one another, even as God in Christ forgave you.

6. Motivation to reach potential - John 14:12 - "Most assuredly, I say to you, he who believes in Me, the works that I do he will do also; and greater works than these he will do, because I go to My Father.

7. Affirmation and praise for accomplishments - 1 Corinthians 3:8 - Now he who plants and he who waters are one, and each one will receive his own reward according to his own labor.

1 Corinthians 3:14 - If anyone's work which he has built on *it* endures, he will receive a reward.

Root System - <u>Other Roots</u>

Psalm 27:10 - When my father and my mother forsake me, Then the LORD will take care of me.

1 John 3:1 - Behold what manner of love the Father has bestowed on us, that we should be called children of God!

Psalm 147:1-3 - Praise the LORD! For it is good to sing praises to our God; For it is pleasant, and praise is beautiful. The LORD builds up Jerusalem; He gathers together the outcasts of Israel. He heals the brokenhearted And binds up their wounds.

Luke 4:18 - " The Spirit of the LORD is upon Me, Because He has anointed Me To preach the gospel to the poor; He has sent Me to heal the brokenhearted, To proclaim liberty to the captives And recovery of sight to the blind, To set at liberty those who are oppressed;

1 John 4:19 - We love Him because He first loved us.

2 Corinthians 6:17-18 - "...I will receive you. I will be a Father to you, And you shall be My sons and daughters, Says the LORD Almighty."

Prayer. "In the name of Jesus, I break agreement with the spirit and stronghold of rejection. I command it to release me and leave me forever. I come into agreement with God, that He loves me with a great love and an everlasting love. He loves me as much as He loves Jesus. Lord, You make me dwell in safety. You have made me accepted in the Beloved, accepted in Christ. You highly value and treasure me. I am Your precious and valuable inheritance. You have already forgiven me for every sin and every mistake because You love me - because You value Your relationship with me. As I believe in You, You also believe in me - that I can do the same works that Jesus did, because You live in me. You see and reward my every thought, word and act of love for You. I receive You as my Father, and You receive me as your beloved son/daughter. I am not an orphan. I am not a religious slave. I am a beloved child and heir. I belong in the family of God. I have a place in God's heart that is mine and mine alone. No one else can take my place in my Father's heart. In the name of Jesus, I take my place in God's heart. I am loved."

Internalized Rejection Strongholds

Romans 5:5 - ...the love of God has been poured out in our hearts by the Holy Spirit who was given to us.

2 Timothy 1:7 - For God has not given us a spirit of fear, but of power and of love and of a sound mind.

Ephesians 3:17 - that Christ may dwell in your hearts through faith; that you, being rooted and grounded in love,

Isaiah 61:1-3 - "The Spirit of the Lord GOD *is* upon Me, Because the LORD has anointed Me To preach good tidings to the poor; He has sent Me to heal the brokenhearted, To proclaim liberty to the captives, And the opening of the prison to *those who are* bound; To proclaim the acceptable year of the LORD, And the day of vengeance of our God; To comfort all who mourn, To console those who mourn in Zion, To give them beauty for ashes, The oil of joy for mourning, The garment of praise for the spirit of heaviness; That they may be called trees of righteousness, The planting of the LORD, that He may be glorified."

Matthew 28:20 - ...and lo, I am with you always, even to the end of the age.

Proverbs 29:25 - The fear of man brings a snare, But whoever trusts in the LORD shall be safe.

Ephesians 4:23-24 - ...and be renewed in the spirit of your mind, and that you put on the new man which was created according to God, in true righteousness and holiness.

Prayer: "In the name of Jesus, I break agreement with all forms of internalized rejection, including poor self-image, low self-esteem, self-rejection and self-hatred. I break agreement with all forms of fear and anxiety and insecurity. I break agreement with inferiority, negativity and suicide. I come into agreement with God that He loves me and accepts me. I will no longer expect rejection or interpret rejection where it does not exist. I take off the old identity, and I put on my new identity as a beloved son/daughter of God. God is healing and restoring me from all forms of brokenheartedness and rejection. God is with me always. I am becoming rooted and grounded in His love for me. I can and will receive His love for me. I can and will love myself. I can and will love others. I can now freely love and freely be loved. I am called, chosen and accepted. I am loved by my Father God, by Jesus, and by the Holy Spirit."

Externalized Rejection Strongholds

Ephesians 4:31-32 - Let all bitterness, wrath, anger, clamor, and evil speaking be put away from you, with all malice. And be kind to one another, tenderhearted, forgiving one another, even as God in Christ forgave you.

Ezekiel 36:26 - I will give you a new heart and put a new spirit within you; I will take the heart of stone out of your flesh and give you a heart of flesh.

James 4:6-7 - But He gives more grace. Therefore He says: *"God resists the proud, but gives grace to the humble."* Therefore submit to God. Resist the devil and he will flee from you.

John 15:12 - This is My commandment, that you love one another as I have loved you.

1 John 4:19 - We love Him, because He first loved us.

Romans 15:7 - Therefore receive one another, just as Christ also received us, to the glory of God.

2 Corinthians 1:3-4 - Blessed *be* the God and Father of our Lord Jesus Christ, the Father of mercies and God of all comfort, who comforts us in all our tribulation, that we may be able to comfort those who are in any trouble, with the comfort with which we ourselves are comforted by God.

Romans 13:1 - Let every soul be subject to the governing authorities. For there is no authority except from God, and the authorities that exist are appointed by God.

Prayer: "In the name of Jesus, I repent of and break agreement with all forms of anger and bitterness and hatred and unforgiveness. I freely forgive others as I have been forgiven. I repent of the mindset that I am a victim or that I have a right to stay angry. I repent of the idea that this world owes me any reparation. I repent of and break agreement with all forms of pride and rebellion and hardness of heart. With God's wisdom, I will honor, respect and have a heart of submission toward the good and loving authority figures that God has put in my life. I will see them as a blessing and not a threat. I repent of and break agreement with hatred, revenge, violence, rage and the spirit of murder. I repent of and break agreement with hurting, harming or abusing anyone around me. I come into agreement with God. I receive love from God, and I will freely love others around me. I receive comfort from God, and I will comfort others. I receive a heart of flesh, a tender new heart from God, instead of a stony heart. As God accepts and values me, I will show acceptance and value towards other people. I am no longer an angry person. I agree with God; I am a loving and forgiving person. I can and will love others as Jesus loves me."

Attempts to Compensate

Hebrews 4:1-10 - Therefore, since a promise remains of entering His rest, let us fear lest any of you seem to have come short of it. For indeed the gospel was preached to us as well as to them; but the word which they heard did not profit them, not being mixed with faith in those who heard *it*. For we who have believed do enter that rest, as He has said: *"So I swore in My wrath, ' They shall not enter My rest,'* "*although* the works were finished from the foundation of the world. For He has spoken in a certain place of the seventh *day* in this way: *"And God rested on the seventh day from all His works";* and again in this *place: "They shall not enter My rest."* Since therefore it remains that some *must* enter it, and those to whom it was first preached did not enter because of disobedience, again He designates a certain day, saying in David, *"Today,"* after such a long time, as it has been said: *"Today, if you will hear His voice, Do not harden your hearts."* For if Joshua had given them rest, then He would not afterward have spoken of another day. There remains therefore a rest for the people of God. For he who has entered His rest has himself also ceased from his works as God *did* from His.

Colossians 2:10 - and you are complete in Him, who is the head of all principality and power.

Romans 5:1-2 - Therefore, having been justified by faith, we have peace with God through our Lord Jesus Christ, through whom also we have access by faith into this grace in which we stand…

Luke 14:11 - For whoever exalts himself will be humbled, and he who humbles himself will be exalted."

Philippians 2:3 - Let nothing be done through selfish ambition or conceit, but in lowliness of mind let each esteem others better than himself.

Prayer: "In the name of Jesus, I break agreement with all forms of striving and struggling to prove my worth to myself, to God and to others. I break agreement with striving to feel important or significant through pride or ego or performance or perfectionism. I break agreement with all forms of competition and comparing myself to others in order to feel accomplished or significant. I break agreement with all forms of religious performance as a means to feel loved or significant or accomplished or important. I come into agreement with God in the finished work of Christ. Right now, I enter into the finished work of Christ. Right now, I find Sabbath-rest in the finished work of Christ. In Christ, I am loved and complete. In Christ, I have peace and acceptance. In Christ, I have significance and importance. I will no longer try to earn something that God has freely given me. I accept and enter into the finished work of Christ: salvation and love and grace and favor."

Sozo pre-appointment information

Thank you for making a Sozo ministry appointment! This information package was designed to help you prepare for your appointment, so that you will get the most out of your ministry session.

What is SOZO ministry?

Sozo ministry was designed to help you overcome and find healing from feelings of rejection and unworthiness, fear and anxiety, anger and bitterness, and other negative emotions. Sozo is a Greek word which is usually translated in the Bible as "save" or "saved". But it means much more than simply being forgiven and someday going to Heaven. It refers to total healing, total freedom, and total wholeness in spirit, soul and body. SOZO ministry was designed for people who are already Christians, already born again, but who are struggling with emotional baggage from the past. This includes your self-image and self-esteem, as well as how you relate to God and others. Sozo ministry was designed to help you in all of these areas.

As a Christian, you have right standing before God because of the finished work of Jesus Christ. You are saved and forgiven. You are a new creation, a born-again prince or princess of God your Father. Nevertheless, you may have emotional baggage and self-image issues from painful childhood experiences, or from traumatic events of the past.

Rejection is the number one issue for most people with emotional baggage of the past. Parental failings and experiences of abuse or neglect or mistreatment cause deep roots of rejection and emptiness, a love deficit, a sense of unworthiness or lack of value. Once established, these roots produce various kinds of fruit in our emotional life, our self-image, and our personality. These fruits are reflected in the three branches of the Rejection Tree diagram: internalized rejection, externalized rejection (or anger), and attempts to compensate (usually by performance). Sozo ministry is designed to help you be healed from the roots of rejection and to replace them with roots of love and acceptance from God. This will produce new kinds of branches and fruits as reflected on the Love Tree diagram.

During your Sozo appointment, the ministry team will lead you through five steps. (Please plan to allow 2-3 hours for your appointment.)

(1.) The first step is forgiveness. You will identify and forgive all the people who have ever caused you to have feelings or roots of rejection. Forgiveness is your key to freedom.

(2.) The second step is inner healing. You will pray with the Sozo ministry team for the healing of your wounded soul. The Bible says that Jesus is the healer of the brokenhearted.

(3.) The third step is repentance. You will identify the fruits of rejection as represented on the branches of the Rejection Tree diagram, and you will "break agreement", or repent of these attitudes and behaviors. Victims usually become victimizers, and then the chain continues. You will break the chain.

(4.) The fourth step is deliverance. The ministry team will lead you through a process of getting rid of any demonic spirits that have gained access to your soul because of rejection issues. It is done in a way that honors you as a person and keeps you in full control of the process, because you have dominion and authority in Christ.

(5.) The fifth step is truth therapy. You will make new agreements in the area of God's love for you. The Bible calls this "renewing the mind". Jesus said, "The truth will make you free."

Pre-appointment preparation

Included in this package is a copy of the Rejection Tree and the Love Tree. You do not have to fill this out before the appointment. You will fill it out with the Sozo ministry team during your appointment. However, it will be good to familiarize yourself with these two diagrams. The Rejection Tree is a symbol of your internal thought life and emotional life. It is a tool that the ministry team will use to help you find healing and freedom. The Love Tree is a symbol of what your spiritual life and emotional life will look like after the Sozo process is complete.

Also included in this package is a short personal spiritual profile of four questions. It is information that is not included on the Rejection Tree, but that the Sozo team will need to help you get completely free. You may answer these questions in advance of your appointment, if you wish. Please know that all of the information that you share in the Sozo ministry session is confidential. Your privacy will be honored and respected.

Post appointment follow-up

After the appointment, you will be given a paper called "Breaking Agreements - Making Agreements". This paper will have scripture verses and prayers for you to use to continue breaking agreement with issues of the past and coming into agreement with God's love for you. It is important for you to use these scriptures and these prayers regularly after your Sozo session until you feel that you are strongly walking in victory and wholeness. You must be committed to your personal healing and victory.

You will also be given a booklet called, "He First Loved Us". This booklet is a great revelation of God's love for you. Please read it and reread it. It will be very healing for you in the Sozo process.

Appointment changes

If for any reason you need to change or cancel your appointment, please call Susie Bieker at 480-813-2021 as far in advance as possible. Susie coordinates Sozo team members for the appointments. Team members sometimes make great sacrifices in order to be available for Sozo ministry sessions. If you need to change or cancel your appointment, please honor the team members' time by calling Susie. Also please make arrangements for childcare if you need to do that. It is very difficult to focus during a Sozo session with children present, with the possible exception of small infants. Thank you!

List and description of "root spirits"

1. **The spirit of infirmity** *(Luke 13:11)* - chronic sickness & weakness, unusual medical conditions

2. **The spirit of fear** *(2 Timothy 1:7)* - insecurity, worry, anxiety, paranoia, insanity

3. **The spirit of divination** *(Acts 16:16-18)* - drugs, witchcraft, astrology, divination, channeling, the occult

4. **The spirit of whoredoms** *(Hosea 4:12)* - fornication and sexual immorality of all kinds, pornography, prostitution, lust for pleasure, money or power, idolatry

5. **The spirit of bondage or slavery** *(Romans 8:15)* - alcoholism, all addictions & addictive tendencies, loss of liberty or self-control

6. **The haughty spirit** *(Proverbs 16:18-19)* - pride, arrogance, bragging, egotism, controlling, critical, judgmental, attitude of superiority, contentious, vain

7. **The perverse spirit** *(Isaiah 19:14)* - all unnatural sexuality such as homosexuality, bestiality, pedophilia, also false and twisted doctrines

8. **The spirit of antichrist** *(1 John 4:3)* - new age or eastern religions, atheism, intellectualism, persecution of Christians and Christianity, blaspheming

9. **The deaf and dumb spirit** *(Mark 9:25-27)* - deafness, muteness, seizures, convulsions, epilepsy

10. **The spirit of heaviness** *(Isaiah 61:3)* - despair, depression, hopelessness, chronic sadness & discouragement

11. **The lying spirit** *(2 Chronicles 18:22)* - lies, deceptions, exaggerations, foolish talking, religious spirits, accusing, wounding with words, cursing people's lives

12. **The spirit of jealousy** *(Numbers 5:14)* - suspicion, jealousy, anger, rage, accusing, competitive, distrustful, heard-hearted, divisive, cruel, hateful

13. **The spirit of stupor or slumber** (Romans 11:8) - spiritually blind or asleep, procrastinating, withdrawn, failure, passivity, fatigue

14. **The spirit of error** *(1 John 4:6)* - false teaching, false belief systems, false world view, false religions, confusion

Other spirits

The spirit of trauma – Demons are bullies. This spirit attaches itself to people at the time of a traumatic event, and causes them to relive that trauma over and over. Cast it out!

The spirit of shame – People who have committed sexual sins or who have experienced sexual victimization will often have a spirit of shame that haunts them with the shame of that event. Cast it out! Then declare over them a restoration of innocence and purity.

The religious spirit – This spirit deceptively impersonates the Holy Spirit. People who have been involved in cults or false teachings often have a religious spirit. People who have had deep inferiority and insecurity issues are very vulnerable to it. It often puffs them up with counterfeit spirituality and false self-importance. Religious spirits also cause legalism, religious pride, and just plain religious weirdness. Help the person to recognize and reject the presence of this spirit…then cast it out!

The spirit of rejection – ALWAYS cast out the spirit of rejection, and with it the spirit of perceived rejection and the fear of rejection. Perceived rejection is a filter that causes the person to reinterpret any communication as rejection, even if it's not. (Lying, stinking devil!) The fear of rejection sets them up for more rejection like a self-fulfilling prophecy.

The spirit of suicide – This is, of course, the spirit that drives people to commit suicide, the ultimate form of self-rejection.

The spirit of death – This spirit is at work if there is a death assignment against someone, evidenced by repeated accidents, brushes with death or attacks on their life through physical health issues. It may also be evidenced by the appearance of death, an attraction to death or preoccupation with death.

The familiar spirit – The familiar spirit operates through mediums, spiritists, and any other form of divination. It is a spirit that knows you and your family history, and will often know things that seemingly no one else could know.

The antichrist spirit – The antichrist spirit is viciously opposed to any form of Christian truth or Christian authority, whether secular or spiritual. It may be associated with new age spirits and practices.

The spirit of witchcraft – This is the spirit that helps you to exercise supernatural power or control from any spiritual source other than God.

Other spirits

The spirit of divination – This spirit helps you seek supernatural guidance or communication from any spirit or source other than God.

Printed in Great Britain
by Amazon